T0107685

Status Symbol

CROSSWORD PUZZLES FOR THE
AUTOMOTIVE ENTHUSIAST

GLEN A. STARKEY

ISBN: 978-1-4669-4111-3 (sc)
ISBN: 978-1-4669-4110-6 (e)

Trafford rev. 06/27/2012

 www.trafford.com

North America & International
toll-free: 1 888 232 4444 (USA & Canada)
phone: 250 383 6864 ♦ fax: 812 355 4082

Status Symbol™   Vol. 1 No. 1

Crossword Puzzles

For the Automotive Enthusiast

PUZZLE EDITOR ~ Joanne McCallum

Editor-in-Chief ~ Glen Starkey

Cover design by

ART & IDEAS STUDIO

Little Rock, AR

COVER PHOTO
1932 Duisenberg
Used with permission of the
Auburn-Cord-Duisenberg Museum
Auburn, Indiana

I will see you again.
Your son,

Glen A. Starkey

Editor-in-chief

A Memorial

This puzzle book is dedicated

To the loving memory of my mother

whose love and encouragement

kept me going

to see it through

to its completion.

Without her support

This book would not

Be possible.

Here's to you, Mom.

I will see you again.

Your son,

Glen A. Starkey

Editor-in-chief

#1

Status Symbol Inc.

ACROSS

3 City in SW Colorado and Old Mexico
4 Symbol for Aries
6 Seeks to beat the winner, space shuttle
8 Be a good one, a game
9 Wagon Train or traveling together
10 Jagged mountain range
14 Soldier with long sword
15 Used in a game with bullseye

DOWN

1 Bold
2 Midwest state north or south
5 Wanderer 1949
7 Small crown
10 Ghost
11 King, queen or the family
12 Thia car says Hi!
13 Snake

#1

Solution:

#2

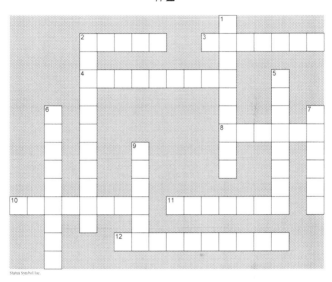

ACROSS

2 Famous CA Lake and resort
3 CA city near Surfer's Point
4 Snow slide
8 African Antelope
10 America's Sportscar
11 One who can discern the trail
12 Famous European Casino

DOWN

1 Movie star or famous person
2 Pathfinder
5 Soldier on horseback
6 Famous resort in Napa Valley, CA
7 Famous beach resort
9 X28 or Z28

#2

Solution:

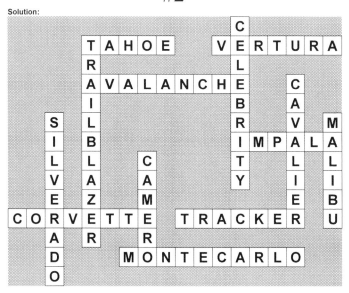

3

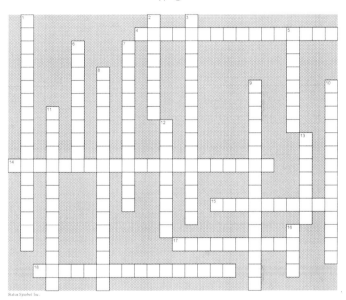

Status Symbol Inc.

ACROSS

4 ONCOMING CARS CANNOT PASS
14 LIGHTED PALM OF HAND AT CROSSWALK
15 SOLID WHITE LINE ON RIGHT
17 GO
18 X ON SIGN OR ROADWAY

DOWN

1 SLOW DOWN AND PROCEED WITH CAUTION
2 STOP
3 NEITHER LANE CAN PASS
5 PAINTED ARROW POINTING LEFT
6 PREPARE TO STOP
7 SOLID BROAD WHITE LINE ACROSS LANE AT SIGNAL
8 LIGHTED WHITE FIGURE WALKING
9 STOP AND PROCEED WITH CAUTION
10 THE LINE BETWEEN LANES .
11 SOLID WHITE LINE OR CURB ON LEFT
12 YELLOW LINE RIGHT OF CENTER LINE,
13 LIGHTED GREEN ARROW
16 OCTAGON ON ROAD OR SIGN

3

Solution:

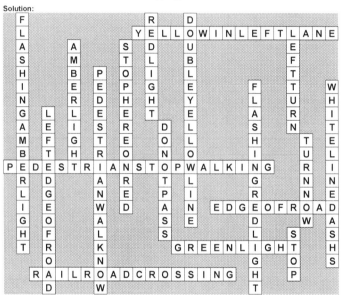

#4

Status Symbol Inc.

ACROSS

2 Gas and distance
6 Shows how fast you are going
8 Ignites fuel
9 Front glass
10 Stopping power
11 Mile keeper
13 Tail light cover
14 Floor covering
15 Opens door
16 Comfort ledge

DOWN

1 Rain sweeper
2 Speed
3 Extra fuel container
4 Gas or clutch
5 Main star of a show
7 Pay without cash
8 Fill up place
10 Rubber loop
12 Drive_____

#4

Solution:

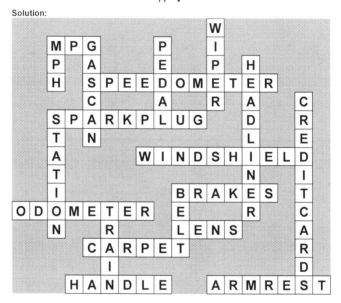

#5

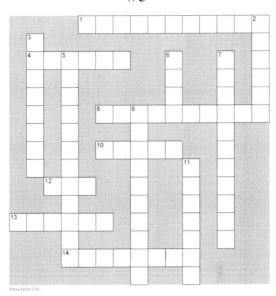

Status Symbol Inc.

ACROSS

1 Increases gas
4 Provides push
8 Charges battery
10 Inflated with air
12 Unlocks/starts motor
13 Energy chamber
14 Coolant container

DOWN

2 Seesaw action
3 Round with teeth
5 Shoots gas
6 Hatch
7 Delivers electricity
9 Shows right or left direction
11 Power supply

#5

Solution:

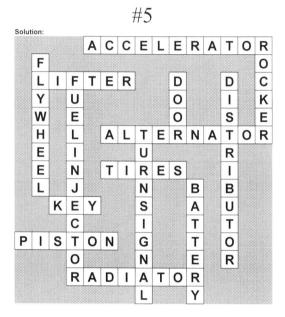

#6

Status Symbol Inc.

ACROSS

3 Nickname for maker of Reliant America
4 Lightweight rope
6 Mustard-colored car for hire
9 A closed-lipped singer
10 Had three headlights
12 French race driver
13 Bird of prey

DOWN

1 Everyman's car
2 Pilgrim's rock
4 A gold one
5 Luxury on wheels
7 Red from Indiana
8 Car for the sands
11 1st all-terrain

#6

Solution:

#7

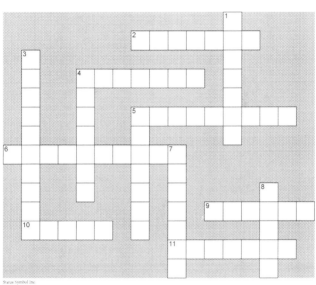

Status Symbol Inc.

ACROSS

2 Feline
4 Songbird
5 Roman soldier
6 Easter parade locale
9 Greek god
10 Kingly
11 French resort area

DOWN

1 "The Sword"
3 Ruler of the highway
4 Bird of prey
5 100 years
7 Girl's name
8 Above all others

#7

Solution:

#8

Status Symbol Inc.

ACROSS

3 Roadside park
5 Octagon shape
7 Wheel cover
8 Hand ice remover
10 Railroad warning
11 Car resting area
13 ____down the runway
14 Drive
15 Diamond shape

DOWN

1 Highway guide
2 Full locomotion unit
4 Early extra seat
6 Cross____
9 _____parking
12 Long luxury

#8

Solution:

#9

Status Symbol Inc.

ACROSS

2 Too fast
6 Extra tire
8 Tags
9 Ignition tools
11 Legal paper
14 Driver's book
15 Learner's
17 Bumper _____
18 Slick stuff
19 Manufacturer
21 Fast start

DOWN

1 Proof of ability
3 Fuel
4 Storage area
5 Highway guide
7 Too close
10 Fuel place
12 Radiator fluid
13 Use to stop
16 Tank up
20 Inflating gas

#9

Solution:

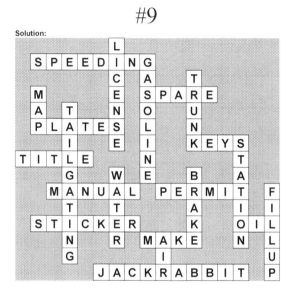

#10

Status Symbol Inc.

ACROSS

1 Get free
3 Indian symbol
5 Second model
7 Zodical bull
9 Earliest Ford
13 Son of Henry
14 Small wild horse
15 Royal and regal

DOWN

2 Shape
3 Musical rhythm
4 Wild horse
6 Trip
8 To sharpen image
10 Searcher
11 Texas cop
12 Official companion

#10

Solution:

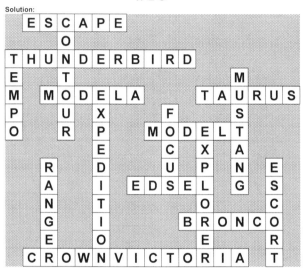

#11

Status Symbol Inc.

ACROSS

2 Starfire
3 Seville
6 Speedwagon
7 Bonneville
11 Taurus
12 Lynx
13 Soft fur, Ford
15 Claw
17 New Yorker

DOWN

1 Rebel
3 Celebrity
4 Pacer
5 Lark
8 Hornet
9 Reliant
10 Eagle
14 Skyhawk
16 Rambler

#11

Solution:

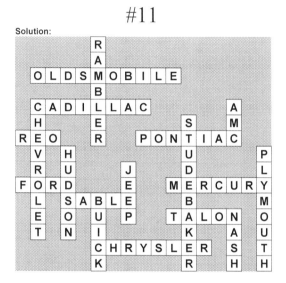

#12

Namesplates

ACROSS

3 Not a train engine
6 Early steam car
7 Planet with rings
8 Of noble blood
9 Had a culrved dash
14 USE's 1st sportscar
15 Sounds like dash
16 A great lake or canal
17 City of gold
18 Rock or a chicken

DOWN

1 A camera lens adjustment
2 Dominates night sky
4 Get away
5 Flying car?
10 "Its a Deusy!"
11 Face on penny
12 French race driver
13 Move out of the way
16 Son of Ford

#12

Namesplates

Solution:

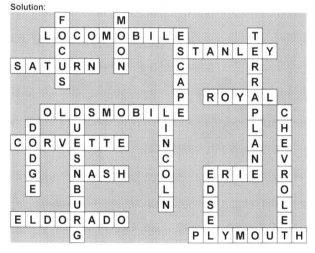

#13

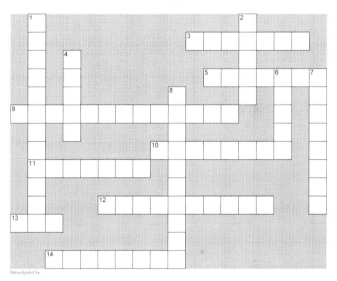

Status Symbol Inc.

ACROSS

3 New Year's is one
5 Fancy Sword
9 Olds 1940 L series
10 Like a fast moving storm
11 4 X 4 Model
12 First car nickname
13 First car's other nickname
14 To arouse interest

DOWN

1 Olds Model 46
2 Custom Cruiser by Olds
4 River flat land
6 2000 model
7 Solar heat
8 Mini Van

#13

Solution:

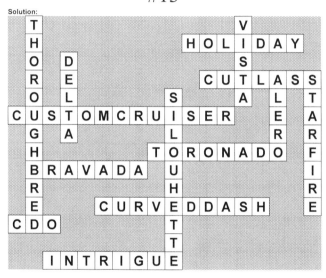

#14

ACROSS

- **3** Speedwagon
- **4** _____of Happiness
- **6** Covered wagon builder
- **10** 32nd US President
- **12** Little Person
- **14** Easter symbol
- **15** Long legged bird
- **16** Of the mainland

DOWN

- **1** Good Luck Insect
- **2** New York river
- **5** Last phase of the moon
- **7** Sweetheart's nickname
- **8** One who jogs
- **9** Opposite of failure
- **11** Honest Abe
- **13** Model by Dodge

#14

Solution:

#15

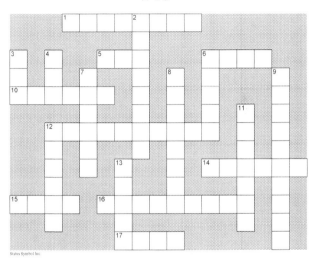

Status Symbol Inc

ACROSS

1 Pay to use
5 Fuel
6 To go on or off the highway
10 Flashing blue or red
12 Advertising
14 Entrance
15 Leaving ramp
16 A highway restaurant
17 Halt

DOWN

2 Highway "oasis"
3 Folded Guide
4 Lubricating fluid
6 Country streets
7 Truck weigh-in
8 Scenic high spot
9 Limited access highway
11 Wheel covers
12 18 wheeler (slang)
13 Natural land areas

#15

Solution:

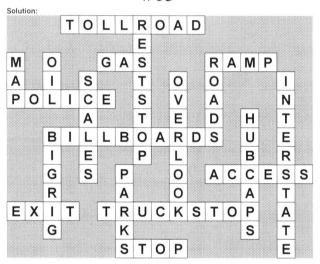

#16

Status Symbol Inc.

ACROSS

2 Police
3 Early Ford nickname
9 Passing lane
10 Get gasoline
11 High beams
13 Restroom stop
15 Set speed
16 Dimmer lights

DOWN

1 Sudden flat tire
2 Fasten seatbelt
4 Police helicopter
5 Inconsiderate driver
6 5 o'clock traffic
7 Go faster
8 Following too close
12 Liquid energy
14 Mustang

#16

Solution:

#17

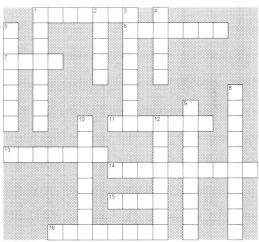

Status Symbol Inc.

ACROSS

1 Sword
6 Storm
7 Exploding star
11 California famous highway
13 French resort
14 First rubber company
15 Brilliant star
16 City of gold

DOWN

1 America's sportscar
2 Rubber Captal of the World
3 Flame of a distant sun
4 Alpha opposite
5 100 Years
8 Gaming resort
9 Racing inspired
10 Burning fowl
12 First front wheel drive since 1937
   Cord

#17

Solution:

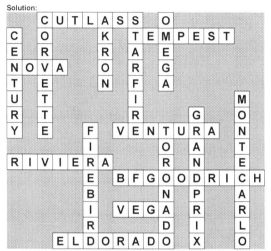

#18

Status Symbol Inc.

ACROSS

3 Oldsmobile
5 Bearcat
7 Recent war vehicle
8 USA's wildcat
9 Elvis had a pink one.
12 USA's 1st sports car
13 1st status symbol

DOWN

1 1st had a curved dash
2 Red from Indiana
4 Astrological ruler of Capricorn
5 Began with wagons
6 A wild pony
10 Honest Abe
11 1st all terrain

#18

Solution:

#19

Traveling Words

Status Symbol Inc.

ACROSS

1 Noon break
3 Direction posted
6 Road work bypass
10 Vacation getaway
11 Group parking place
12 Road atlas
13 Counter post
18 Scenic vista
19 Red in rear

DOWN

2 Motor cover
4 Highway system
5 Lock companion
7 Break place
8 Leisure trip plan
9 Warning sticks
14 Vacation traveler
15 Road over water
16 Hot to go
17 Sleep building

#19

Traveling Words

Solution:

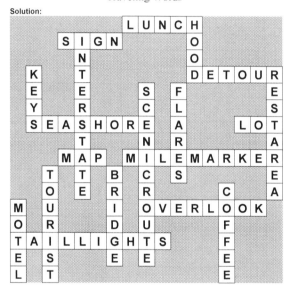

#20

"Under the hood"

Status Symbol Inc.

ACROSS

2 Sparkplug measure
4 Regulates spark
7 Activates engine
9 Winter driving aids
10 Mover of air
11 Similar to pipes
13 Powerplant
15 Tire layer
16 Ignites gas

DOWN

1 Power source
3 Fluid measurer
4 Cool breezes
5 Keeps dirt from entering the engine
6 Coolant tank
8 Circulates coolant
10 Delivers fuel
12 Lubricating fluid mover
14 Warm in winter

#20

"Under the hood"

Solution:

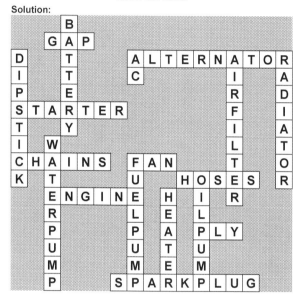

#21

Status Symbol Inc.

ACROSS

3 Lifts car
7 Gas saver gear
10 Front see through
11 Controls speed and direction
14 Backup gear
16 Nut remover
17 Extra tire

DOWN

1 Opens and closes
2 ___ Flaps
4 State required
5 Car rescue vehicle
6 Clear glass
8 Front amber lights
9 Required for driving
12 Winter tire aid
13 Frost remover
15 Speed ____

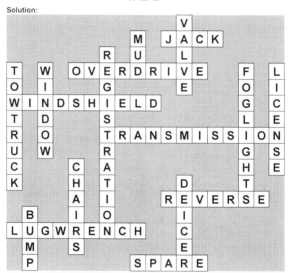

#21

Solution:

#22

"A" car names

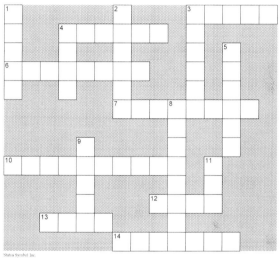

Status Symbol Inc.

ACROSS

3 Built by Pearce
4 Red
6 Made in Kokomo, IN
7 Ocean
10 U.S. Representative
12 Top or best
13 Powder cleanser
14 Model by Dodge

DOWN

1 Book of maps
2 Goddess of the dawn
3 Texas capital city
4 Also a city in Iowa
5 Model by Ford
8 U.S. citizen
9 "Of the stars"
11 Highest trump card

#22

"A" car names

Solution:

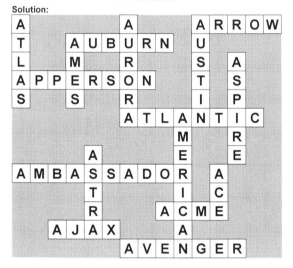

#23

"B" car names

Status Symbol Inc.

ACROSS

1 Red Cross donation
2 "Clear as a ____"
4 Dollar
5 Mountain lion
6 Loan officer
7 War boat
11 Symbol of happiness
12 Kind of pear

DOWN

1 Enclave model maker
2 Very early car
3 California built car
4 Built by Stutz
5 Model by Pontiac
7 Animal on nickel
8 Makes pies and cakes
9 Honey maker
10 Flies and chirps

#23

"B" car names

Solution:

#24

"Car" car names

Status Symbol Inc.

ACROSS

1 24 in a____
3 Nat King ____
4 Baby bear
5 Chevrolet model 1937
6 Solid gold ____
8 ____roads
10 Winner (nickname)
11 Half man, half horse
12 Big heavy duty gun
13 High society membership

DOWN

1 By Chevrolet
2 Defeats all
3 A unit of wood
4 New contestant
6 CA island resort
7 22nd president
9 Mighty ____ had struck out
10 Rent a boat

#24

"Car" car names

Solution:

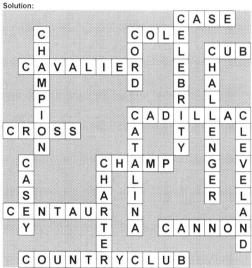

#25

"D" Car Names

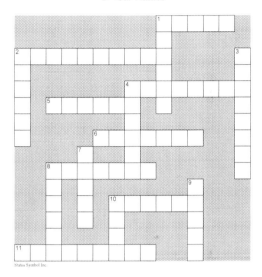

Status Symbol Inc.

ACROSS

1 Nickname of luxury car
2 Built by Durant
4 Home of the Ford car
5 Charles (Early Mfgr)
6 Motor city
8 Term of endearment
10 Spanish explorer
11 Native of Detroit

DOWN

1 Blond movie star
2 Also built the Duesy
3 Famoous race horse
4 Cyclecar of Ohio
7 Male duck
8 American chemical corporation
9 To move out of the way
10 Model by Dodge

#25

"D" Car Names

Solution:

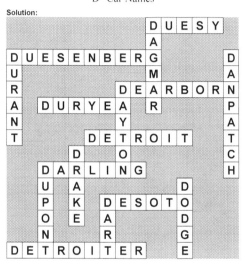

#26

"E" Car Names

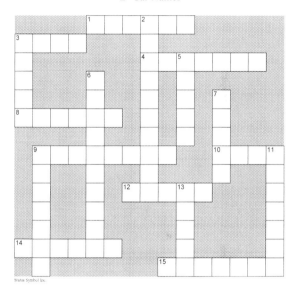

Status Symbol Inc.

ACROSS

- **1** "I have found it!"
- **3** "Duke of ____"
- **4** Cincinnati OH car
- **8** Light bulb Inventor
- **9** Cadillac model
- **10** A great lake
- **12** County in England
- **14** Kingdom
- **15** South Bend, IN car

DOWN

- **2** Belongs to all
- **3** U.S. Symbol
- **5** Also a fine watch
- **6** Frugal auto
- **7** Mr. Fudd's first name
- **9** Financial balance
- **11** Total cover
- **13** Car from Elkhart, IN

#26

"E" Car Names

Solution:

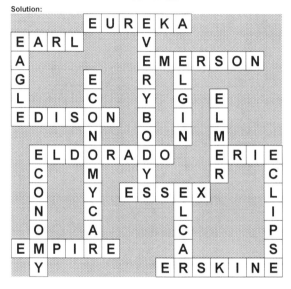

27

ACROSS

7 Oldsmobile F_____
8 Dodge C_____
9 Oldsmobile A_____
11 Chevy Hybrid
13 Checrolet G_____
15 Buick R_____
17 GMC Hybrid
18 Chevrolet "famous person"

DOWN

1 Pontiac F____
2 Saturn
3 Pontiac A____
4 "French" Pontiac
5 Get away
6 Oldsmobile F_____
7 Merge together
10 DeSoto F_____
12 Oldsmobile B_____
14 Chevrolet "little truck"
16 Pontiac A____

27

Solution:

#28

"F" car names

Status Symbol Inc.

ACROSS

- **2** Other Chevrolet body style
- **4** Contains more
- **5** Action to cool off
- **6** Chevrolet body style
- **8** Rich man's magazine
- **9** Quick
- **10** "_____of men"
- **11** Hunted with dogs
- **12** Built Model A

DOWN

- **1** Style
- **3** Of the U.S. government
- **5** Substitute for parent
- **6** Cadillac body style from Pennsylvania
- **7** Carnival wheel ride
- **8** He who waves it

#28
"F" car names

Solution:

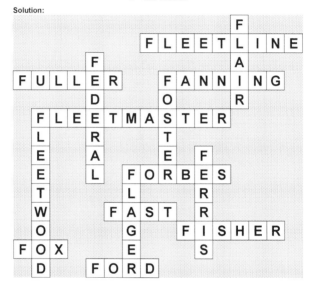

#29

"G" car names

Status Symbol Inc.

ACROSS

1 Paul Gaeth's car
2 Studebaker
4 Peace meeting city
6 This car is a GP (with a hyphen)
8 Level of wind force
11 Racing dog
12 Ball
13 To move smoothly
14 Without shift

DOWN

1 Higher than colonel
2 Archangel with horn
3 Dial showing gas in tank
5 Cartoon cat
7 Skydiver yell
8 Precious jewel
9 Fuel on the move
10 He who plants

#29

"G" car names

Solution:

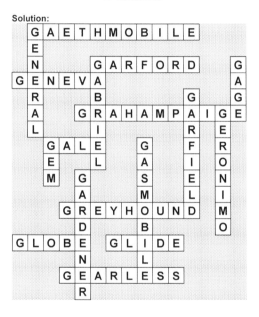

30

"H" Car Names

Status Symbol Inc.

ACROSS

1 Not from low land
3 Model by Kaiser
4 Dwelling place
5 House walkway
6 Center of wheel
7 New York river
9 Famous hotel chain
10 He who hikes up
11 Sherlock

DOWN

2 "Horsey _____"
3 Head covering
5 Model by Hudson
6 Robert Hupp's car
7 "_____s & McCoys"
8 The VIII king
9 Opposite of valley

30
"H" Car Names

Solution:

#31

"I" Car Names

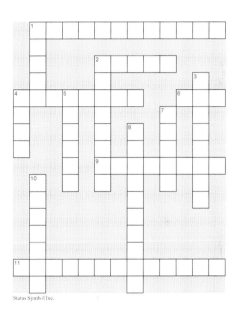

Status Symbol Inc.

ACROSS

1 July holiday
2 Henry I. Innes' car
4 Northern state
6 Little Devil
9 Bold and fearless
11 Global

DOWN

1 Perfect
2 Fierce Indians
3 Of an empire
4 "Hawkeye State"
5 Native American
7 E.A. Myers' car
8 Across state lines
10 "Hoosier State"

#31

"I" Car Names

Solution:

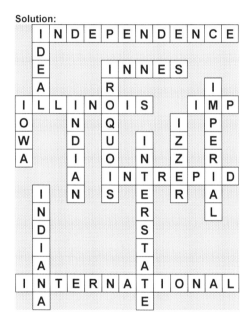

#32

"J" Car Names

Status Symbol Inc.

ACROSS

2 Fast bunny
3 7th U.S. President
6 Duesenberg model
7 GMC model
9 AMC model
11 Biblical river
12 Lyndon B. _____
14 Same as famous tea

DOWN

1 Child's game
3 Of Julius Caesar
4 "Home, _____"
5 "Stupefyin'" _____
6 Army vehicle
7 Named after dad
8 1952 airplane car
10 Built by Ray Saidel
13 Built by John E. Meyer

#32
"J" Car Names

Solution:

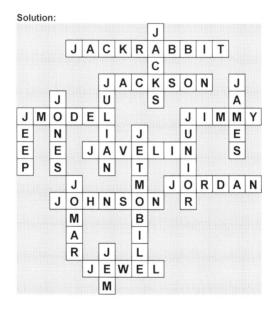

#33

"K" Vehicle Names

Status Symbol Inc.

ACROSS

1 Plain gelatin brand
3 Doctor of "The Fugitive" TV show
4 Beaverton, PA car
5 Colonel on "Hogan's Heros" TV show
7 Built the Manhattan
8 Term for early New York
10 Truck by Chevrolet
11 Built by two women
12 Philadelphia, PA car

DOWN

1 Omaha, NE car
2 Large MO city
3 Famous applicance brand
4 Andy of "Taxi" TV show
6 KK
7 Region of the Yukon
8 34th U.S. president
9 Mankato, MN car

#33

"K" Vehicle Names

Solution:

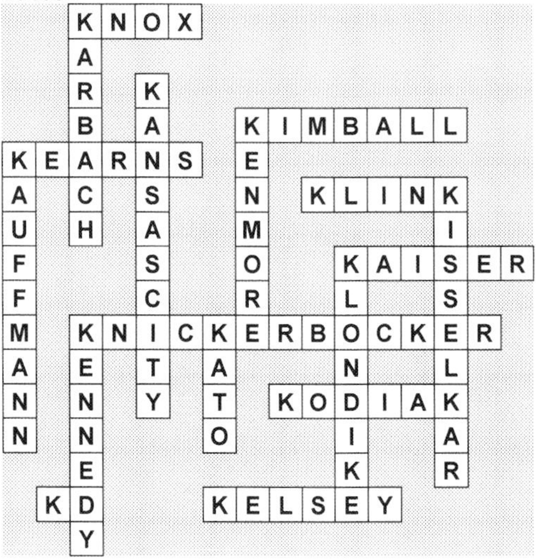

#34

"L" Car Names

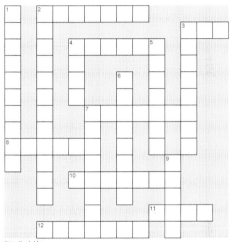

Status Symbol Inc.

ACROSS

2 Shore leave
3 Legal rule
4 Victorious wreath
7 Honest Abe
8 Shows the way
10 French explorer
11 King of beasts
12 "Big Blue ____"

DOWN

1 Crazy car?
2 Not close
3 Brand of laundry bluing
4 Wildcat
5 Built by Buick
6 Texas nickname
7 Girl's name
9 Jerry ____ Telethon

#34

"L" Car Names

Solution:

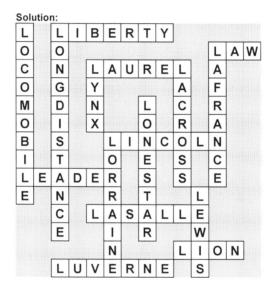

#35

"M" Car Names

Status Symbol Inc.

ACROSS

4 Telegraph code
7 Man of high country
9 Bill of "Ghostbusters"
12 Purple swallow (bird)
13 Jack Benny's car
14 Major attraction

DOWN

1 Rules the night sky
2 Planet next to the sun
3 Computer screen
5 Dept. store car
6 Not a comet
7 ____tri-car
8 Public news
10 5th U.S. president
11 Rotary engine car

#35

"M" Car Names

Solution:

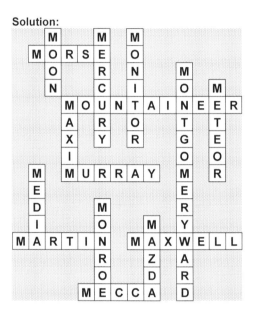

#36

"N" Car Names

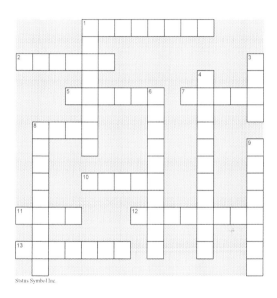

Ststus Symbol Inc.

ACROSS

1 Opposite of southern
2 Next ten years
5 Ozzie or Harriett
7 Dodge SE 4x2
8 Exploding star
10 Allentown, PA car
11 Built the Rambler
12 Federal
13 Ohio car

DOWN

1 1956 dream car
3 Dodge model
4 Huge waterfall / 3+1=__
6 NE U.S. electric car
8 Built by Lincoln
9 General of France

#36
"N" Car Names

Solution:

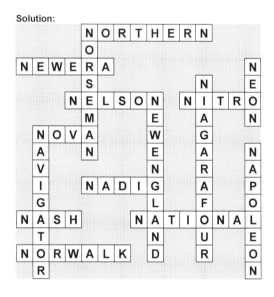

#37

"O" Car Names

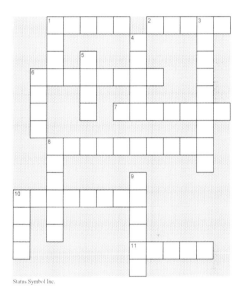

Status Symbol Inc.

ACROSS

1 NY Car, group leaves
2 Actor Wells
6 Competitor in games
7 ____Bay Bridge
8 Built Aurora
10 Wagon trail to the west
11 Oldsmobile model

DOWN

1 Precious gem
3 Model by Saturn
4 City near Boystown
5 Model by Dodge
6 Columbus is the capitol
8 Land of the east
9 Toledo, OH car
10 Single

#37
"O" Car Names

Solution:

#38

"P" Car Names

Status Symbol Inc.

ACROSS

1 Sneaky thief
3 Avenue, Famous street
4 Ford model
5 Indian pony
6 AMC model
9 1954 Plymouth model
10 Wagon train rider
12 Without error
13 Model by Chrysler
14 Built the Arrow model

DOWN

1 Loyal to country
2 Built the Firebird
3 He who finds the way
4 Built Hawk model
7 Pilgrim's rock
8 Without equal
11 Has rotary engine
13 Cooking utensil

#38
"P" Car Names

Solution:

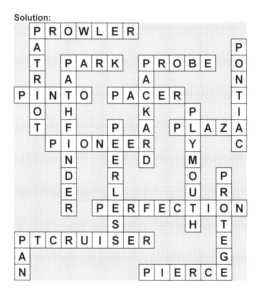

#39

"Q & U" Car Names

Status Symbol Inc.

ACROSS

1 Sport _____ Vehicle
3 Fast
4 Colcord _____ , 1905 car
7 Boston, MA car
8 Electric car by Fisker
12 1902 car from PA

DOWN

1 Intended for all
2 American small, open auto
4 Extreme or beyond
5 America
6 Neward JN car
9 Chevrolet
10 Merged
11 King's mate

#39

"Q & U" Car Names

Solution:

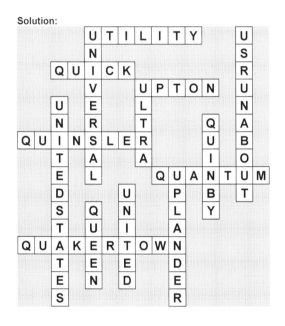

#40

"R" Car Names

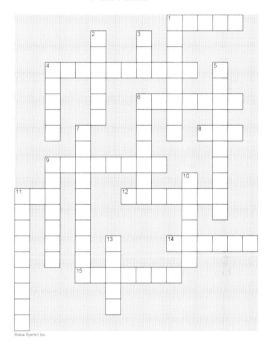

Status Symbol Inc.

ACROSS

1 Resists authority
4 To meet
6 Dependable
8 Speedwagon\
9 Chevy model
11 Animal symbol for Aries
12 Running amuck
14 Buick sportscar
15 Model by Oldsmobile

DOWN

1 A form of government
2 Very early small car
3 ____4
4 Quick like water
5 Sport Vehicle
6 French resort area
7 Model by Buick
9 Model by Nash
10 Forest caretaker
11 ____ Dart
13 Kingly

#40

"R" Car Names

Solution:

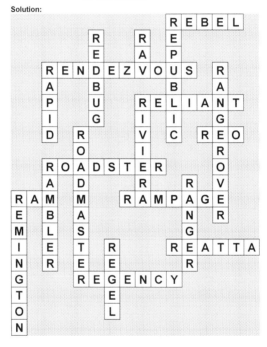

#41

"S" Car Names

ACROSS

1 Star flame
2 By Plymouth
3 Ford Falcon
4 Model by Geo
7 Radiant fowl
9 Bird of prey
10 Chrysler model
12 Avanti builder
14 Model by Geo
15 Model by GMC
16 Ringed planet
17 Singing bird
18 Larger cab PU

DOWN

1 Dodge model
2 Sexy Sun sign
3 Dept store car
4 Dark image
5 Solar rhythm
6 Mercury model
8 City edge
9 Model by Buick
10 Journey in jungle
11 Desert
12 Group Roomy
13 By Jeep
14 Model by Dodge
15 Cadillac model

#41

"S" Car Names

Solution:

#42

"T" Car Names

Status Symbol Inc.

ACROSS

1 Indian symbol by Ford
2 Yellow jewel
3 Resort lake, Chevrolet model
4 Pontiac sports model
9 26th US President
11 Mercury model
13 Makes new path
14 Model by Pontiac

DOWN

1 Had 3 headlights
2 Musical beat
3 Follows the trail
5 Native of the Lone Star state
6 Ford's big seller
7 Lincoln model
8 Good report
10 "Bull" star group
12 Eagle claw

#42

"T" Car Names

Solution:

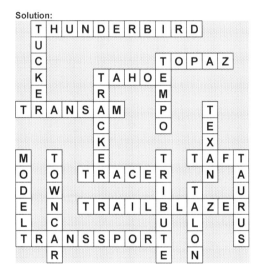

#43

"V & W" Car Names

Status Symbol Inc.

ACROSS

1 Small town native
2 Built by Ford
3 Winner
4 By Chevrolet
5 Undertaking
7 Trees
8 Alexander ___
9 By Plymouth
12 By Jeep
14 Small fast dog
15 Quiver, slang

DOWN

1 Enclosed truck
2 Jeep model
3 Dream
4 Built in 1909 -1929
6 Space probe
9 Snake
10 By GMC
11 Vale
13 Not black

#43
"V & W" Car Names

Solution:

#44

"X,Y, & Z" Car Names

Status Symbol Inc.

ACROSS

3 Model by Lincoln
4 Auburn, IN 1908 -15 car
5 Northerner
6 Lock or university
7 John G. _____ ,1900
10 Willis Copeland & Schuyler ___
11 Built in Ohio

DOWN

1 Oshkosh, WI car
2 Alaska territory
4 Rollin forerunner
6 Car for hire
8 Quick or fast
9 Model by Chevrolet
10 1900 car Marion, OH

#44
"X,Y, & Z" Car Names

Solution:

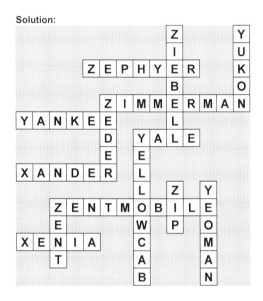

45

Auto ID (US only)

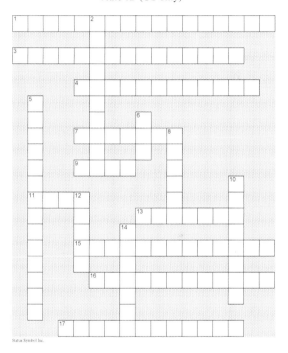

Status Symbol Inc.

ACROSS

1 10th characturer in VIN
3 First digit in VIN is
4 2nd character in the VIN
7 L in 2nd postion
9 J in 2nd position
11 F in 2nd position
13 Z in 2nd position
15 G in 2nd position
16 1 in first position
17 4 or 5 in first position

DOWN

2 N in 2nd position
5 I in VIN stands for
6 These are not found in the VIN
8 N in VIN stands for
10 P in 2nd position
12 B in 2nd position
14 V in VIN stands for.

45

Auto ID (US only)

Solution:

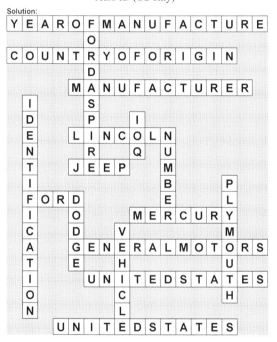

#46

TV and Movies.

ACROSS

1 "Nash Bridges"
9 "Route 66"
12 "Back to the Future"
15 Ad slogan "In my Merry _____"
16 "Back to the Future", 2nd car

DOWN

1 "Christine"
2 "Vegas" 1957 car
3 "Dobie Gillis"
4 Green Hornet's 1966 car
5 "Blues Brothers"
6 Batmobile was a 1955

7 Dinah Shore sings an invitation.
8 Kit on "Knightrider"
10 "The Andy Griffith Show"
11 1928 car, "My Mother the Car"
13 Jack Benny drove this.
14 Cars on "Mayberry"

#46

TV and Movies.

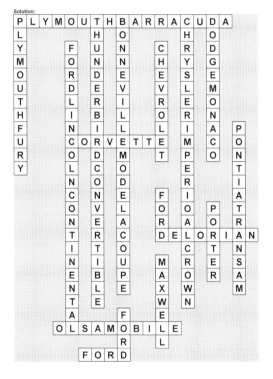

#47

State Slogans

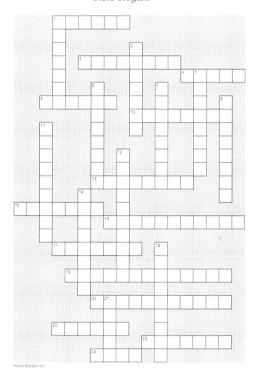

Status Symbol Inc.

ACROSS

1 Last Frontier
3 Old Line State
4 Pine Tree State
8 Aloha State
10 First State
13 Prairie State
15 Peach State

16 Constitution State
17 Grand Canyon State
19 Bay State
20 Magnolia State
22 Sunflower State
23 Hoosier State
24 Hawleye State

DOWN

1 Yellowhamer State
2 Sunshine State
5 Natural State
6 Show Me State
7 Centenial State
9 Bluegrass State
11 North Star State
12 Golden State
14 Wolverine State
18 Pelican State
21 Gem State

#47

State Slogans

Solution:

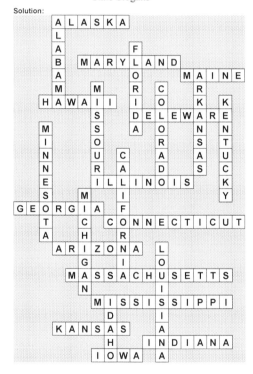

48

State Slogans ~ Part 2 (Some states have more then one.)

ACROSS

1 Badger State
5 Cornhusker State
6 Garden State
7 Peace Garden State
8 Empire State
12 Buckeye State
15 District
16 Sagebrush State
19 Green Mountain State
20 Evergreen State
27 Old Colony State
28 Land of Enchantment
29 Heart of Dixie

DOWN

2 Beaver State
3 Sooner State
4 Mountain State
6 Silver State
7 Old North State
9 Keystone State
10 Old Dominion State
11 Ocean State
13 Mount Rushmore State
14 Palmetto State
17 Granite State
18 Great Lakes State
20 Equality State
21 Flickertail State
22 Volunteer State
23 Crossroads of America
24 Beehive State
25 Treasure State
26 Lone Star State

48

State Slogans ~ Part 2 (Some states have more then one.)

Solution:

W	I	S	C	O	N	S	I	N								O			W
			R				N	E	B	R	A	S	K	A		L			E
N	E	W	J	E	R	S	E	Y								L			S
E			G				N	O	R	T	H	D	A	K	O	T	A		
V			O				O						H			O			V
E			N	E	W	Y	O	R	K				O			M			I
D							T						M			A			R
A		P		V			H						A				O	H	I	O
	R	E		I			C					S				N			
	H	N		R			A				S		O			I			
	O	N		G			R			S		O				I			
	D	I	S	T	R	I	C	T	O	F	C	O	L	U	M	B	I	A
	E	Y		N			L			U		T						
	I	L		I			I			T		H						
	S	V		A			N			H		D						
	L	A					A			C		A						
	A	N	E	V	A	D	A			A		K		N				
	N	I								R		O		E				
	D	A		M		V	E	R	M	O	N	T		W				
				I						L		A		H				
				C						I				A				
		W	A	S	H	I	N	G	T	O	N			M				
		Y		I			O		E		A			P				
		O		G			R		N					S				
I		M		A			T		N		U			H		M			
N		I		N			H		E		T			I		O			
D		N					D		E		A			R		N			
I		G	T		M	A	S	S	A	C	H	U	S	E	T	T	S		
A			E			K		S								A			
N	E	W	M	E	X	I	C	O		E						N			
A			A			T			A	L	A	B	A	M	A				
			S			A													

49

Hybrid & Electric Cars

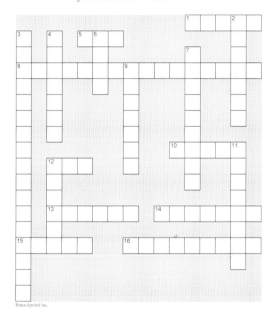

Status Symbol Inc.

ACROSS

1 Chrysler
5 Dodge Pickup Hybrid
8 EV1
10 Chevrolet _____Hybrid
12 Lincoln ~ sport version
13 Chevrolet E85, uses Flex Fuel
14 Jack Benny's car
15 Chevrolet 4 wheel drive subcompact
16 Chevrolet Pickup E85

DOWN

2 Alternative fuel made from corn
3 Runs on Hydrogen
4 Dodge pickup
6 Chevrolet smallest hybrid
7 Chevrolet Hybrid Pickup
9 Chevrolet 4 cycl. with "eco" button
11 Cadillac
12 Chevy _____ Hybrid

49

Hybrid & Electric Cars

Solution:

```
                              A S P E N
C   D   R A M                         T
H   U   V           S                 H
E A R L Y E L E C T R I C C A R
V   A   O   Q       L       N
R   N       U       V       O
O   G       I       E       L
L   O       N       R
E           O     T A H O E
T   M K Z   X       D     S
F   A               O     C
U   L                     A
E   I M P A L A   M A X W E L L
L   B                     A
C R U Z E     S I L V E R A D O
E                         E
L
L
```

#50

Name that Vehicle!

Status Symbol Inc.

ACROSS

2 Kingly
6 Curved Dash
7 Avoid being hit
8 Sheep's head insignia
9 Indian good luck symbol
13 Car company that built an airplane
15 REO
17 Headlight in center of grill
19 Nash
21 American Motors Corporation
22 Horse
23 Built by two women
24 Rock

DOWN

1 Makes music with mouth closed
3 Bowtie insignia
4 "Jimmy"
5 To cross the stream
10 "Hi" (TV commercial)
11 Indian
12 Towncar
14 Army Vehicle
16 AMC
18 First Oldsmobile model
20 Explorer

#50

Name that Vehicle!

Solution:

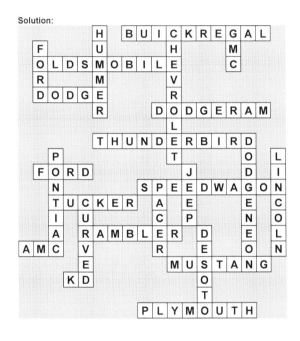

#51

Automobile Trivia

Status Symbol Inc.

ACROSS

1 2 Car companies merged in 1955
5 Owned department store chain before investing in cars.
7 Location of first US traffic light
8 Last one built in 1966.
10 First fast food drive thru 1951
11 Who started the assembly line for cars?
13 This one ended in 1986
14 First commercial use of electric vehicles in 1897
15 Last one built in 1966
16 Christened by Amelia Arhart
17 Sport inspired by bootleggers running from the law.

DOWN

2 Held the land speed record until 1900
3 First car with step down into design.
4 First gasoline-electric hybrid in 1917 in Chicago
6 Who perfected the assembly line for cars?
9 Inventor of 3 color stop light
12 Last one built in 1959

#51

Automobile Trivia

Solution:

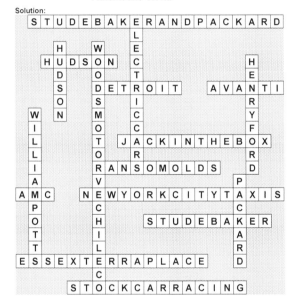

#52

Presidential cars

Status Symbol Inc.

ACROSS

5 This armored car first belonged to this guy. FDR rode in it to give his "Infamy" speech.

8 FDR'S favorite V-12 car's nickname

12 This president ordered the first car with the "Bubbletop".

13 Herbert Hoover's 1932 car

14 1921 Pres. Harding's car

DOWN

1 First civilian car built after production resumed following war effort.

2 Pres. Reagen rode this in his birthday parade.

3 1st president to ride a car to his Inauguaration.

4 1993 Pres. Kennedy's car in Dallas

6 Pres. Bush took this 2006 car to England with him

7 FDR'S 1939 favorite car.

#52

Presidential cars

Solution:

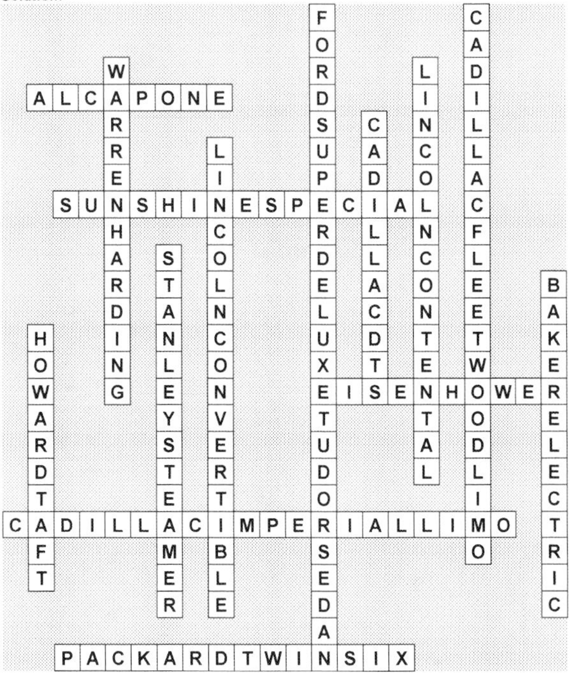
FORDSUPERDELUXETUDORSEDAN
CADILLACFLEETWOODLIMO
WARRENHARDING
ALCAPONE
LINCOLNCONTINENTAL
CADILLACDT
LINCOLNCONVERTIBLE
SUNSHINESPECIAL
STANLEYSTEAMER
BAKERELECTRIC
HOWARDTAFT
EISENHOWER
CADILLACIMPERIALLIMO
PACKARDTWINSIX